Angel Star

Tatterdemalion Blue

New Edition
Published by **Tatterdemalion** Blue in 2025

A CIP catalogue record for this book is available from the British Library

Cover design and layout by **Tatterdemalion** Blue

ISBN 978-1-915123-09-1

Tatterdemalion Blue
74 Maxwell Place
Stirling
FK8 1JU

www.tatterdemalionblue.com

Angel Star

Written by John King

Illustrated by Emma Turley

~ For Adrian & Matthew ~

Angel Star

Angel Star

There was a boy who one day found

A ladder to the stars upon the ground

With rung upon rung of burnished gold

Such a sight did his eyes behold

Angel Star

And as he gazed so high above

To his eyes appeared a soul-white Dove

So soul-bright like a star ablaze

His secret wish was to fly Her Way

Angel Star

When all of a sudden and all too soon

She shone in the rays

Of the Sun and Moon

And there above him way way far

Shone the Light of an Angel Star

He gazed and gazed upon Her Light

Wishing to go there if he might

Angel Star

For upon the rungs of burnished gold

He must now climb that he may behold

Her wingéd flight

Her Light

Her Love

Upon his journey to the Star above

Angel Star

"*Where to begin?*

When to start?"

He asked these questions

Of his Heart

Angel Star

"*What will happen?*

What will I find?"

He asked these questions

Of his Mind

Angel Star

When all of a sudden a bright flame shone

Shining in his heart and mind as one

And the golden rays from up above

Flew down to greet him as a soul-white Dove

Angel Star

And then said a Voice so calm so clear

"Do not be afraid I am always here

For the Light of Love of the Angel Star

Within your Silence is where you are

So place your feet upon golden rungs

And know your journey is just begun"

Angel Star

And with his feet he seemed to fly

Silent footsteps in the sky

Past clouds and skies so swiftly far

To the Sun

And the Moon

And the Angel Star

Angel Star

And here he shone as the soul-white Dove

In silent joy and light and love

Where desire in his imagination grew

Before his eyes for now he knew

"The Light of Love of the Angel Star

  Within your Silence is where you are"

Angel Star

So if to the stars a ladder you find

Awakening desire in your heart and mind

And somewhere up there way way far

You see the Light of an Angel Star

Listen to Her Voice

To Her Words so fair

And your guided footsteps

Will take you there

www.ingramcontent.com/pod-product-compliance
Lightning Source LLC
LaVergne TN
LVRC092041070426
835508LV00006B/309